Cori,
thank you for your
kindness! Love,
Love, Mama Beast

D1532645

SECRET KINDNESS AGENTS:

How Small Acts of Kindness
Really Can Change the World

FERIAL PEARSON

Published by WriteLife
(An imprint of Boutique of Quality Books Publishing Company)
www.writelife.com

Cover Artwork: ©Kristy Stark Knapp

Printed in the United States of America

ISBN 978-1-60808-091-5 (p)
ISBN 978-1-60808-108-0 (e)

First Edition

TABLE OF CONTENTS

IN MEMORIAM
By Sarah Edwards

Emily Dickinson was wrong. Hope is not a "thing with feathers." Hope is a verb.

It was in December when Avielle was murdered. At first, I didn't use the word "murder" because a murder doesn't happen in a space dedicated to math problems and art projects. Murders don't exist in a noisy hallway where friends shout weekend plans and leave behind tiny bits of paper and forgotten pencils. Murder does not belong in a school. Schools hold the promise of our nation. Lives are not taken in a school. My best friend's daughter could not possibly be a victim of a school shooting.

Avielle remains in my mind as I last saw her — bouncy brown curls that defied control framing her laughing eyes. She was running across a grassy field holding my daughter's hand while my son raced after them with a bat and ball. While the adults sat on the porch watching a rumbling thunderstorm pass on the horizon, our kids invented their own version of a baseball game that involved sliding in the mud as often as possible. We talked about how our kids attended such amazing schools. The academics were far beyond what we'd learned at their age. The teachers were helping our kids learn how to contribute as part of a community.

Community matters to Avielle's parents. Within hours of the shooting, the national community was headed for their front door. We couldn't get there fast enough. As the plane sat on the tarmac waiting to take off, I looked out the window trying to avoid conversation with the man sitting next to me. I didn't want to talk about why I was crying. Minutes into the flight, he handed me his coat and said, "You're shaking." I covered my legs and mumbled an embarrassed, "Thank you." Halfway into the flight, I got up the courage to speak and said I was going to Newtown. My best friend lived in Sandy Hook. The rest of the flight we talked in hushed tones, asking questions that had no answers. As we stood to gather our things and leave the plane, I handed him his coat, but the stranger refused to take it. He insisted that I keep it as I continued on my way to Newtown. I remember this random act of kindness from the first few hours after the shooting. The man wanted to do something to help.

Mounds of stuffed teddy bears and a warehouse full of cards attest to a nation, and indeed, a world full of people who felt the need to surround Newtown with a blanket of kindness. Deep within us is the need to respond. Just as the laws of physics teach us that every action has an equal and opposite reaction, this grossly horrific event prompted tens of thousands of people to react in an overwhelming response of hope. Hope is a verb.

Much like the students who acted in this book, we must celebrate opportunities to actively support and assist each other as members of a community. As a teacher, I have dedicated my professional life to building classroom communities; Avielle's murder in a school was a personal call to action.

Avielle's mother and I were those little girls shouting in the halls forty years ago. We have a lifetime of being friends of the best kind. We value moments like our kids playing in the rain. We celebrate the classrooms that actively hope for change. For Avielle's parents, their hope has been forged in a steely resolve to have a conversation around the need for everyone to belong in a community. This means researching brain health and considering how we build a society where every member is a valued part of the whole. Check out the organization for yourself at www.aviellefoundation.org to consider what your hope looks like in action.

FOREWORD
By Daniel Boster

As a long-time high school teacher, I've spent a great deal of time reflecting on the lives of schools. It will surprise no one who is a part of the life of a school — a teacher, a student, a member of the staff — if I were to tell them the days that make up the life of any school are complicated, messy, and hectic. I imagine that even people who don't spend a lot of time in schools are at least vaguely aware of this. But, what people who are "on the outside" don't often see is that the lives of schools are also often marked by beauty, grace, and quiet moments of inspiration. For every story of violence, abuse, bullying, and tragedy in schools that splash across television news tickers and social media feeds, there are just as many, perhaps more, narratives of hope, resilience, dignity, and, yes, kindness.

I teach at the school where Ferial Pearson and these young Secret Kindness Agents did their work during the 2012-2013 school year. In addition, I'm currently teaching them in a literature class during their final year in high school. This brings me to the reason I'm so excited that Ferial asked me to contribute a small piece to this project.

To begin, I simply really like all of the folks involved in this project. For them, "kindness" is not simply a "project" to be assigned, reflected upon, and dismissed. While I'm pretty sure all of them were kind before the tragedy of Sandy Hook and Ferial's bringing this idea to them, I do believe that carrying out

conscious acts of kindness changed these students. They truly are some of the most considerate students I've ever worked with. They are gentle in their being and pleasant to be with in a classroom. Now, is this project solely responsible for this? Probably not, but, as their reflections make clear, it did make a difference. They all came to see the value in these small deeds. The smiles that lingered on their faces afterward showed evidence of their joy. They embraced the feeling of having done something good. They allowed themselves to feel empathy and to be vulnerable in acts of service. A project that allows students to accomplish all this can be counted a success. However, that's not all it did.

As you read, one of the items on their initial list of acts to begin the project is "Help someone carry a heavy load." Based on what some of the students wrote about, for them, this item was about actually helping someone physically carry something. Of course, this is a nice act of kindness. Yet, as I read this list, my mind kept returning to that simple phrase — help someone carry a heavy load. There is no doubt that young people today carry heavy loads. At our school (and most others), the heavy load takes as many forms as there are students. We walk around clearly daunted by these heavy loads that interfere with our ability to learn, to enjoy our lives, to simply be. Often, our burdens seem overwhelming to us. We may even be tempted to give up, to put the heavy load down and walk away.

I like to think that all of the acts these students did — the monetary gifts, the kind words, the smiles, the whiteboard cleaning — were small steps in the process of lessening those loads. Can these acts erase hardship, cure a school or a society of its ills? Of course not. But, a project like this can make a few young people more conscious of the loads that other people carry and inspire them to take action rather than letting others simply struggle on their lonely paths. I know that they made some of their fellow classmates feel lighter, happier, and better.

In our culture, where the idea of practicing acts of kindness can be turned into a meaningless slogan on a bumper sticker, these students decided to act. The skeptics among us may be tempted to say things like: "So what?" or "There will be another shooting," or "What about all the people you didn't help?" These are reasonable things to wonder. I do, myself, now and again, but I like to think I know how these

students might answer. It might go something like this, "We know we can't make everything perfect, but we are trying to make things better. We are trying to *be* better." This answer can give us a great deal of hope and inspire us to be more kind.

I'm humbled and proud to contribute to this book because I believe that it's important for us to proclaim this work. These students tell their stories as a way to both celebrate what has already happened and as a promise of the great things they will surely do.

INTRODUCTION

Saruman believes it is only great power that can hold evil in check, but that is not what I have found.
I found it is the small everyday deeds of ordinary folk that keep the darkness at bay.
Small acts of kindness and love. — Gandalf - J.R.R. Tolkien, The Hobbit

As a mother of a first-grader and a teacher of students who have been bullied to the breaking point, the tragedy at Sandy Hook Elementary School in Newtown, Connecticut, shook me to the core. I wanted to keep my children home with me under a giant blanket on the couch where I could keep us safe. I knew the excruciating pain the parents and the rest of the Newtown community felt, but then it occurred to me that the shooter must have been suffering, too, to do what he had done. When people hurt me, I always feel that they are lashing out from a place of pain and insecurity. More than anything, I feel helpless, powerless, and very scared.

As I talked with my six-year-old daughter and nine-year-old son about the tragedy, they kept asking me why someone would cause such devastation. My daughter suggested that if people had been kinder to him, maybe things would have turned out differently. My son said that he got angry when people bullied him, and he'd want to fight back, but then someone would be kind to him, and this would help. Naïve and simple, maybe, but I wondered if there was something to these comments.

My husband reminded me that the one place where I feel hopeful, even powerful, when I have lost a little faith in humanity, is the classroom as I talk with students. When I studied at the University of Nebraska at Omaha for my Master's Degree, I discovered the work of Brazilian educator Paolo Freire, who was instrumental in the idea of "problem-posing" education, where students and teachers alike identify problems in their communities and work together to solve them through dialogue, followed by action and reflection, repeating the cycle. Whenever I came up against a wall in teaching, I would ask myself, "What would Freire do?" and the answer would come through the hearts and minds of my students and help me over and around that barrier. Well, here was a wall if ever there was one. I knew I had to go to my students, pose the problem, have some kind of dialogue with them, and together we would figure out the action and reflection that would bring some light to the darkness of this tragedy.

Later that week, as I self-medicated with my Pinterest addiction, I found an idea to have "Secret Agent" envelopes distributed to students with random acts of kindness assignments in them. Again, I thought what if people had been kinder to the shooter? Is it possible that compassion could have prevented the tragedy? What if we could prevent such a tragedy in the future by making our school a kinder place? We can never know for sure, but in a time when I felt so helpless, this idea gave me a small feeling of power, and I decided to present the idea to my students when we got back from winter break. They knew what it was to feel helpless and powerless, to be the bullied and the bully, to be angry, but also to be the recipient of kindness. I wondered if they were familiar with the warmth and joy that comes with spreading kindness. Could they discover some modicum of power and happiness within themselves? I did have some sneaky teacher hopes. I hoped they would spread kindness, that it would help build community and a feeling of family in the classroom, that students would build a habit of kindness, develop more empathy, know what compassion looks like, and that they would become addicted to how good it feels to be caring. Despite my hopes, I couldn't have dreamed or been more surprised by what was about to happen. This book is the story of how we tried to keep the darkness at bay and how our lives changed in a million tiny ways in the process.

TOP SECRET

WEEK ONE

No act of kindness, no matter how small, is ever wasted. — Aesop

After winter break, I brought up the tragedy at Sandy Hook in class with my juniors and asked if they had anything they wanted to say about how they felt, and what they were thinking. They had many of the same questions, feelings, and thoughts that my own children had. I shared my feelings about losing faith in humanity after I had read the news, but I knew from looking at their faces there was still an abundance of good left in the world. I shared what my children said with them and about the idea of kindness changing the world, one small bit at a time. They seemed intrigued. I brought up the idea about Secret Kindness envelopes with random assignments inside that I saw on Pinterest and said I would have envelopes ready; if they wanted one, they could get one and complete the assignment, and then, I would give them a small prize. We talked about what kindness looks like and came up with a few examples of things we could do. I gave them a chance to talk among themselves and brought it up again the next time we met.

What happened next blew my mind. They said, "If we're going to do this, we're going to do it right. We don't want prizes, and we don't want this to be just once in a while. We'll do this every week, and we'll ALL do it." My mind whirled with how much work this was going to entail, the logistics, the details.

They had answers for everything, of course!

We had twenty-one people in the class, so we created a list of twenty-one acts of kindness that the students could complete. My only conditions were that they had to be things that didn't require money or resources other than time and energy, and they had to be completed within the confines of the school. If they needed help getting something to someone anonymously, I would help them deliver it, and if they wanted to add candy or a treat as a bonus, I would provide that as well so that they wouldn't have to spend any of their own money on this project. We debated whether or not things should be done anonymously, and we decided that they should, whenever possible. After a brief brainstorming session on the whiteboard and slips of paper that they turned in with three ideas each, we had a final list:

SECRET KINDNESS AGENT ASSIGNMENTS

- Sit by and talk to someone who is always alone at lunch or in study hall.
- Stay after class for two minutes to help a teacher clean up and straighten desks.
- Help someone carry a heavy load.
- Smile and make eye contact with everyone you see for at least three days.
- Give an honest and real compliment to someone you don't usually talk to at school and make it about personality and character instead of appearance.
- Donate clean and gently used clothing you (or friends and family) no longer need to the school nurse and school social worker for students who may need them.
- Eat lunch with or hang out with a special needs student at school.
- Help out teachers and other staff members who have full hands in the hallway.
- Sit somewhere different at lunch at least three days this week.
- Write a letter of appreciation to a student at school about all the good things you've seen them do. This student should be someone people don't usually notice.
- Help someone who is struggling with homework or classwork at least once this week.

13

- Write a thank you note to a teacher listing all the things he or she has done for you or other students and/or the reasons why you look up to him or her. Bonus: add a treat or candy to the note and leave it when the teacher is not looking.
- Write a thank you note to the janitors telling them how much you admire and appreciate their work. Bonus: add treats or candy and leave it for them in the main office.
- Write a thank you note to all of the office secretaries listing the reasons why you appreciate them. Bonus: add treats or candy and leave it for them when they're not looking.
- Write a thank you note to an administrator and list things you admire about him or her. Bonus: add a treat or candy to the note and leave it for him or her anonymously.
- Write a thank you note to a guidance counselor and list all the things he or she has done for you. Bonus: add a treat or candy to it and leave it anonymously.
- Offer to help a teacher hand out papers and erase/write on the board for them as he or she teaches.
- Pick up litter inside and outside the school for half-an-hour after school for at least three days.
- Make IOUs for staff members that they can cash in to have you clean/scrape ice and snow off their car after school.
- Find out who is celebrating their birthday in the month (teachers, staff, students…it's up to you) and make them birthday cards with an optional treat inside. Try to find someone who may not be the most popular or likely to celebrate his or her birthday with others. Leave it anonymously.

WEEK TWO

You never know when a moment and a few sincere words can have an impact on a life. — Zig Ziglar

I created twenty-one envelopes and put one of the assignments in each, and each envelope had a number from one to twenty-one on it. I picked a cheesy song to play ("We Are the World") and went into class with my heart pounding. What if they changed their minds? What if they talked to their friends about it and decided it was a dumb idea?

That didn't happen. Instead, they wanted to take it to the next level and create an oath that we would recite every week when we picked our envelopes. They also wanted to make a list of risks that we were taking in doing this project. After some fascinating discussion about *The Green Lantern*, rhyme schemes, abbreviation, consensus, some small group work and then coming back as a large group, here's what they created:

SECRET KINDNESS AGENT OATH

I accept wholeheartedly, every day
To fulfill my kindly duties
In the most secret way
No good act, no kindness shall escape my sight
Beware our kindness; S.K.A.'S MIGHT!!!

SECRET KINDNESS AGENT RISKS

• People may mock me for being nice.
• People may think I'm a nice person.
• My face may hurt from smiling too much.
• I may not get thanked.
• People may question my sanity.
• I may become a happier person.

I played "We Are the World," as they all picked a random envelope in silence, wrote their names on it, copied the assignment in a secret place, and put the envelope back on my desk. We each held up our hands in or own styles and recited the oath and the risks. Class went on as usual, and they were on their own in the school, spreading kindness. By the time class was over, my face hurt from smiling, and I was questioning my own sanity while already feeling happier myself. Maybe there was something to those risks!

WEEK THREE ONWARD

Kindness in words creates confidence. Kindness in thinking creates profoundness.
Kindness in giving creates love. — Lao Tzu

We only spent fifteen minutes a week on the Secret Kindness Agents project for the next few weeks. Of course, being my Freirian self, I knew there had to be reflection after the action in order for students to internalize and reap the benefits of what they accomplished, so at the end of every week, students took ten minutes to write a journal response, answering a few questions to hand in:

- Describe what happened.

- What did you think and feel about what happened?

- What was your mood like before you completed the assignment?

- What was your mood like after you completed the assignment?

We repeated the ceremony of playing a social justice song (and I had no end of suggestions from the students), picking an envelope, writing down the assignment, reciting the oath and risks, and then moving on with class as usual. It took only a few minutes.

I saw smiles on some faces as they wrote. Some struggled with putting real emotions down on paper, but they did it anyway. They took it seriously. They held their heads up high when they handed them in. I felt humbled by their courage. The darkness was starting to lift.

CASSIE'S RIPPLE EFFECT

No kind action ever stops with itself. One kind action leads to another.
Good example is followed. A single act of kindness throws out roots in all directions,
and the roots spring up and make new trees. The greatest work that kindness does to others
is that it makes them kind themselves. — Amelia Earhart

Cassie was one of the quietest and most hard-working members of our class. In addition to being a full time student, she worked full time at a local fast food restaurant and walked there every single day after school to work until close. She saved up $6,400 in cash to buy herself a car and had enough left over for registration, gas, insurance, and more. Talk about resilience, persistence, and determination!

Cassie also had one of the biggest hearts in the class. A few weeks into our project, Cassie asked me privately if she could do something that wasn't in one of the envelopes; she wanted to give $25 of her own money to a student who was not the most academically gifted, but who worked hard, wanted a better future, and who maybe flew under the radar. I argued with her and said I wouldn't feel right letting her give away her own money, and I would give the $25. She refused (turns out, she's stubborn, too), I gave in, so we compromised. I matched her donation, and we gave two gifts of $25.

Together, we crafted an email to the staff that asked them to nominate a student who fit Cassie's criteria and explained what we were planning to do. Some staff members emailed back within a day, and I had three other staff members donate $25 each, raising our number of gifts to five. One teacher wrote back and said she had been Cassie's teacher the year before and was proud of her progress; Cassie was describing herself a year ago!

Later that day, I posted on Facebook about how proud I was of Cassie (I didn't mention her name) and described her plan. By the end of the week, I had four more donations: one from a local attorney, a professor at the university, and a co-worker. A fellow Freedom Writer teacher, who was unemployed at the time, sent cash by mail and asked that I make sure it went to a teen parent or a foster child. In the end, we had nine gifts and nine nominations. Cassie's face nearly split open, her smile was so big, when I told her about the ripple effect her idea had on other people.

We went to work figuring out how to distribute the money. Cassie wanted it to be anonymous, and she wanted it to be a complete surprise. Students at the school receive yellow notes calling them down to the office, usually because they are in trouble, and Cassie thought that these would be a great decoy. We spent an hour after school creating the gift envelopes. We typed up the following note for each student and put them in the envelopes along with $25 cash:

Dear _____ _____,

Even though you don't think that people notice your hard work, we want you to know that we do notice. You are special and deserving of good things, and we hope that your future is bright. This money is for you only. You can spend it on yourself, and not on anyone else.

From The Secret Kindness Agents

Cassie decorated each envelope, and together we stuffed them, sealed them, and handed them to Mrs. Lewis in the main office, who had the brilliant idea to tell the recipients to open them there so she could recycle the paper. Cassie wanted to split them up into as many different days as possible so that her "happiness could be spread out" when she was watching them open their envelopes. She loved watching their reactions, and we heard reports from staff members around the school about the huge impact those envelopes had on the people who received them. There was disbelief, tears, shock, and gigantic grins. One student read the note in the office, then was seen reading it again in the library, and again in his classroom. Cassie couldn't stop smiling, and neither could I.

WE WERE IN THE NEWS!

Too often we underestimate the power of a touch, a smile, a kind word,
a listening ear, an honest compliment, or the smallest act of caring,
all of which have the potential to turn a life around. — Leo Buscaglia

Word spread about Cassie's kindness, and soon, there was a news article about the Secret Kindness Agents in the *Ralston Recorder*, the local newspaper, written by Adam Klinker, an alumnus of the school, and published on May 8, 2013. Here is that story. <u>Reprinted with permission from *The Omaha World-Herald.*</u>

AGENTS FOR GOOD
by Adam Klinker

Who are these doers of delights? These furtive philanthropists? These sub-rosa stowers of sweetness?

Random acts of kindness come into our lives so seldom some students at Ralston High School decided to take some of the randomness out of them.

Students in the Avenue Scholars program at RHS, led by their teacher Ferial Pearson, helped devise a system whereby they could more purposefully shine a little light into others' days.

They've become known as the Secret Kindness Agents and in their two months on the prowl, they've spread their message far and wide and are breaking their silence to serve as a reminder we can all help spread the love.

"A lot of people say 'Don't sweat the small stuff,' and I've never understood why," said junior Avenue Scholar Maribel Navarrete. "The small things often make the most difference in a person's life. A small crack in a foundation can lead to major problems."

Pearson said she had been meditating on the subject of kindness in the wake of December's school shooting at Sandy Hook Elementary School in Newtown, Conn., that claimed the lives of 26 people — 20 of them children.

The perpetrator of the shooting, Adam Lanza, has been portrayed in the media as an angry, embittered loner.

"I had been thinking a lot over break about Sandy Hook and wondered if there had been more kindness in Adam Lanza's life if it could have been prevented," Pearson said. "I saw on Pinterest an idea where you give your students secret assignment envelopes with random acts of kindness in them and suggested to the students when we got back from break that I have the envelopes, and whoever wanted to do one could take one."

To that end, the students built steadily on small things in hopes of creating a big scene at RHS.

The students took to the envelopes with vigor, and before long, had created more secret acts they could do, came up with an oath for the Secret Kindness Agents and have made the selection of an envelope a ceremony in itself.

The students now ply their secret doings once a week and also write in their journals about their feelings on what they do.

"It feels good," said junior Ernie Moran. "I did something for (Spanish teacher) Mrs. (Kim) Zeleny and she gave me a hug. It makes you feel all warm and fuzzy inside to make someone's day and know they're feeling good, too."

The Avenue Scholars continue to add to their altruistic repertoire.

They've sat with someone who was previously sitting all alone, struck up conversations with people whom they don't normally talk, given anonymous birthday cards, left encouraging notes for students and teachers.

Junior Kendra Story added to the body of good works when she herself got a lift from a total stranger who scraped her car's windows after one of the winter's many storms.

"It made my day," Story said. "To know that there was still a nice person out there who cares and would do something like that gave me a good feeling."

While the little things added up, junior Caslyn Lange also saw an opportunity to create a somewhat bigger splash.

Using her own money and also finding help from several donors, Lange decided she would give nine $25 mini-grants to deserving students at the school.

She had teachers nominate the most deserving students, based on such criteria as classroom effort and attendance.

"It wasn't necessarily for the kids with the highest grades but we did want it to be someone who tries really hard and might just need a little help," Lange said.

"I wanted it to be for kids who have hope so that I could give them even more hope. I wanted to say to them, 'Don't give up just because you might not have money.' I wanted to say, 'A lot of people care about you.'"

Lange and Pearson worked together to select the finalists, and on distribution day, Lange sat quietly and inconspicuously in the RHS main office and watched as, one by one, the nine recipients of the money received a decorated envelope with $25 inside.

"I was supposed to be the bad kid waiting to see the principal," Lange said of her incognito special agent role in waiting. "It was fun to watch and I was happy to see it happen. A lot of people were really surprised by what they found in the envelope."

Pearson said Lange's thinking outside the box on the secret agents project provided a measure of validation in the assignment.

"When Caslyn wanted to do her special assignment that was not one of the ones in the envelopes, I knew that something had clicked in class, and it made all of the work worth it," she said.

THE AGENTS

Never doubt that a small group of thoughtful, committed citizens can change the world.
Indeed, it is the only thing that ever has. — Margaret Mead

Of course, you can't be a secret agent until you have a secret agent name. This was a serious issue that needed to be addressed immediately, according to my Agents. A few years ago, my students nicknamed me "The Beast," to which I initially took offense. They explained, however, that in "teen speak" someone who is a beast is a person who is good at what they do, so I accepted the compliment and the nickname. It followed me to my new school by word of mouth, and when I got to this class, it became "Mama Beast," as the students also saw me as a parental figure; they decided that would obviously be my S.K.A. name. Although I called them my Baby Beasts, they did need their own individual agent names. They were able to pick their own names based on their own personal characteristics, and while some needed help from the class, most knew exactly what they wanted.

The funniest moment was when we named Marlon "Biggie," and Caslyn came in late from an orthodontist appointment. Marlon is well over six feet tall, and Cassie is tiny. She stood next to "Biggie" and looked up at him.

"What should I be?" she asked him.

"Smalls!" I shouted.

"Too soon, Miss. Too soon," said Ernie, without skipping a beat. Look up Biggie Smalls if you don't know who he is.

At the end of the year, Cindy Grady, the publisher of this book, came to class to help us pick the organization to which we would donate any net proceeds from its printing. The students already nominated organizations that meant something to each of them, and then we narrowed the choices down to the following organizations that were put to a secret ballot vote when Cindy joined us:

- Inclusive Communities (to provide scholarships for students to attend IncluCity Camp in Omaha)
- Make a Wish Foundation
- Humane Society
- Juvenile Diabetes Research Foundation
- Siena Francis House (for the homeless in Omaha)
- Dysautonomia Foundation
- Mosaic (for people with mental illness)

Cindy tallied up the votes and announced that the Juvenile Diabetes Research Foundation had won the majority of votes. Our S.K.A. agent who found out earlier that year he was diabetic was overjoyed, as was the whole class.

Then, we took pictures of each student against the whiteboard, and the rest of the students wrote words around each person to describe them. (Thanks again, Pinterest!) They even made Cindy have her picture taken and wrote words around her, despite having just met her. They had no problem coming up with positive words about each other, about celebrating the winning organization, about welcoming Cindy with open arms, and as I watched them I realized they all knew so much about each other, cared about each other, and maybe even loved each other as family. Freire's work had definitely happened here.

CASLYN LANGE - S.K.A. "SMALLS"

> *Remember, there's no such thing as a small act of kindness.*
> *Every act creates a ripple with no logical end. — Scott Adams*

A girl was helping me with my worksheet, and when we were finished, I said, "Thanks for all the help. It was very nice of you. Thank you for your patience, too." I laughed. I was nervous before I did it, but the words kind of came out. I liked the feeling and it was really cool to be able to make someone's day better. It's good to be kind to people who are nice, because they probably don't get as much attention as they deserve. Because of my act of kindness, she probably won't mind helping me out again when I need it.

One time, there was this girl, a sophomore, I think, walking down the hall. She dropped $40 on the ground and didn't realize it. I picked it up, and the kid next to me saw it and said, "Oh, it's your lucky day!" I ran up to her, tapped her on the shoulder, and told her she dropped it. She smiled and said, "Thank you so much!" and I said, "You're welcome," and walked away. I know it was not an assignment, and I didn't know it was going to happen. It just got thrown in front of me. My classmate's reaction made me realize that not very many people would have given it back. Her reaction made me realize that more people should do nice things like that; she must not have had many good things happen to her because she was SO surprised. I was proud of myself and was hoping for good karma in the days to come.

MACKENZIE CARLSON - S.K.A. "CHEEZY"

The fragrance always stays in the hand that gives the rose. — Hada Bejar

It wasn't until I received my second assignment that I got into the spirit of the idea. I had to write a letter to a school official I had spent the most time with and had really gotten to know. I had always heard harsh things about this official, but when I got to know her, I was shocked about how kind and caring she was. She is the 'go to girl,' the one who gets things done and makes sure the rules are followed, and I respect her for that. She always asked how my classes were going and how my day was, and she always cared about my high school experience. I wrote her a letter telling her how much I appreciated all she has done for me and thanked her for being so helpful. I was sick and didn't feel good that day, but then I really felt exhilarated and happy after writing the letter. I hoped this act would change the school by giving the administrators confidence and change their perception of how students see them.

Another time, I was trying to figure out what janitor I should write a note to. I decided to write to Matt Z., because he is really nice and always tries his best. When I gave it to his mom to give to him, she told me that he had had a bad day, and this was my chance to make him feel proud of his work. I was nervous because I was scared he would find out that I was the one who gave him the letter, but I was excited that I could help someone. I felt happy almost instantly afterwards and glad that I could help him feel good about himself. I was hopeful that my kindness would rub off on others.

AYELE DALMEIDA - S.K.A. "A. CAT"

Wherever there is a human being, there is an opportunity for kindness. — Seneca

The first time I started doing the S.K.A. assignments, I was really embarrassed and wanted to quit doing them. People were confused because I had never been nice to them before. But the new kids I sat with were really nice to me, and we all talked about different things and got to know each other. After we finished the project, I felt so great, because this was the first time I had ever done anything like that. I was so proud of myself, because I did not quit even though people were mocking me. People thought I was going crazy, like when I was picking up trash, and they had no idea what I was doing. The most important thing I gained from doing this assignment was to always believe in myself, and no matter how bad life can get or what people may say, I will never quit, even if I think I can't handle it.

After the project, I was a totally different person, because my parent was proud of me, all my friends were proud of me, and so were my teachers. The only thing that mattered to me was what they said. As long as they had my back, I could do anything. For the first time in my life I felt appreciated, and I felt proud of myself because of the way I helped people.

KASHYA BURRELL - S.K.A. "KASH-YEAH"

Let us always meet each other with smile, for the smile is the beginning of love. — Mother Teresa

Honestly, I don't have a favorite act. I enjoyed being able to do just about anything. I was able to smile at someone in the hallway more often, and starting conversations with others made me feel more accomplished. I felt like I was making a difference in their lives. It didn't change my thoughts dramatically at first, until the end, when I stopped smiling at people. I felt boring and almost alone, even though I was with people, so I started smiling and talking to people again, and I felt better. Not only did this positively affect the ones I talked to, but it also positively affected me. I hope that by me doing little things like smiling and talking to others, they will also want to make an effort to talk to other people. Not only will they make someone else's day better, but also their day will become better.

One time I approached a different table in the cafeteria and the girls stared at me. I set my tray down and went to get ketchup. I came back and the girls looked at me again in confusion until one said, "Why are you here?" I said I needed to sit at another table for the day. After that, they welcomed me with open arms. We sat, ate, and talked. It was a blast, and afterwards, I noticed I was in a better mood. It was neat and a new experience for me to be able to be myself and not put on a mask.

FERIAL PEARSON

ADRIAN DIAZ - S.K.A. "SPIKEY"

It is the characteristic of the magnanimous man to ask no favor
but to be ready to do kindness to others. — Aristotle

I wrote a letter to one of my favorite teachers and left it on her desk with a Snickers candy bar. I was worried about how I was going to put the letter on her desk without her knowing it was me, but I did it and was proud of myself. I think my teacher liked the Snickers bar better than the letter. NO! Just playing. She liked the letter, but she didn't know who it was from, so that made it better.

MARIBEL NAVARRETE - S.K.A. "CHI"

Hatred, jealousy and excessive attachment cause suffering and agitation.
I feel compassion can help us overcome these disturbances and let us return to a calm state of mind.
Compassion is not just being kind to your friend. That involves attachment because it is based on
expectation. Compassion is when you do something good without any expectations –
based on realizing that "the other person is also just like me." – Dalai Lama

---

Knowing that you are the reason for someone else having a good day after it started as a bad one gives you a feeling that not many people will understand. However, I live for that feeling! When I was little, I remember telling my mom about what I wanted to be, and she tells me now that all I've ever wanted to do was help people. Doing this assignment reminded me of that passion that I have for people. Before this, I was losing a lot of faith in humanity because let's face it…the world is cruel. So when we had the opportunity to get a grade for just being a good person, it made me smile. Then we got the assignments, and the students in my class were just as excited as I was, and that made me wonder how many other people would love to do things like this.

For one of my assignments I had to smile at everyone I saw. I didn't smile much anymore, so doing this assignment made my jaw hurt…A LOT! I liked it, though, because not a lot of people smile anymore, so when I saw all the smiling faces coming back at me, it made me feel great.

LAUREN JOHNSON - S.K.A. "BUTTERFLY"

What sunshine is to flowers, smiles are to humanity. These are but trifles, to be sure;
but scattered along life's pathway, the good they do is inconceivable. — Joseph Addison

I helped someone carry a heavy load. I always do that, but it made me feel good anyway and proud of myself. I also wrote a note to one of the administrators and put it on their desk. In the note, I thanked them for everything good they do for the school. I feel like I did something really nice and good. I was nervous, I wanted them to like it, but eventually I felt good about myself because I know that I made someone's day.

LANCE OTTO - S.K.A. "SCRAPPY DOO"

> *As long as we observe love for others and respect for their rights and dignity in our daily lives, then whether we are learned or unlearned, whether we believe in the Buddha or God, follow some religion or none at all, as long as we have compassion for others and conduct ourselves with restraint out of a sense of responsibility, there is no doubt we will be happy." — Dalai Lama*

I was having a bad morning, but I stayed after class before I went to lunch and organized the laptop cart. This kept my mind busy for a while, and as I was putting the last few laptops in, the teacher told me to go to lunch...LOL. She cracks me up. I felt appreciated for helping her out. She was stuck on making me go to lunch, but I wanted to finish what I started. I felt good for helping out and trying to take some responsibility for my class's inability to put things back where they belong.

Another time, I picked up litter after school for thirty minutes. I started in my last period class, picking stuff up from the floor. When I was cleaning, I got some weird looks and glances. I just kept working on my S.K.A. assignment. I thought I was going to get made fun of, but I felt great about what happened next. I got thanked a couple of times, which was nice, and made me feel like I was appreciated. It was good to know people sometimes see kindness. It made me feel excited to get my next assignment and to see how it would turn out!

FERIAL PEARSON

NICK REVIA - S.K.A. "SLICK"

Forget injuries; never forget kindness. — Confucius

I was having an okay day, and then I saw one of my teachers carrying a big box, so I offered to take it and carry it to her room. I felt really good about what I had done and I liked helping someone who needed it. Afterward, I felt happy. Another time, I wrote a letter to the attendance lady, Mrs. Jones. I felt really good about what I wrote and how it might affect her. I also picked up litter around the school. I think I picked up mostly everything and was proud of myself for doing a good job. I was kind of in a bad mood before that, but after seeing the results of my hard work, I felt better.

RACHAEL EVANS - S.K.A. "REVANS"

He who sows courtesy reaps friendship, and he who plants kindness gathers love. — St. Basil

There were a lot of acts that I liked and enjoyed doing, but I would have to say that my absolute favorite Secret Kindness Act was writing a letter to one of my teachers thanking her for all that she has done for me. In my time at school, I have only had three teachers who I feel actually cared about not only my education, but about me. They were and still are there for me when I am down and need someone to talk to. It is very rare to find a teacher who you can click with the way I did with mine. So, I guess what I am saying here is to treat your teachers with respect and when you find teachers you connect with, hold on to them.

I hope that everyone catches on to what we have done and takes it above and beyond school. Take kindness out into the real world, and you never know, just a smile, a wave, or even an acknowledgement could change someone's whole day. Step outside of your comfort zone and say, "Hi" to someone you don't normally talk to, donate a dollar to the homeless, and go beyond the bounds of what you're used to doing. You could change the world.

ERNESTO "ERNIE" MORAN - S.K.A. "LIGHTNING/VOLTIC"

Kindness is gladdening the hearts of those who are traveling
the dark journey with us. — Henri-Frederic Amiel

I wasn't sure how I was going to help in the beginning, so I helped a friend with their math homework, which made me feel good and smart. Another day, I saw a teacher moving a cart full of things, so I opened the door to his classroom for him. He thanked me and told me I was nice and a hard worker, and that made me feel awesome. Then, I sat at three different tables at lunch. It was interesting to make new friends and talk to people I haven't talked to in a long time. I was nervous that people would judge me, but it felt good after a while and it was nice to meet new people. I told a teacher I'd clean out her car. She hugged me and laughed, saying I was sweet. It was cool seeing her reaction, I was truly happy to see how I brightened her day — it made me feel all warm and fuzzy inside.

JESUS RODRIGUEZ - S.K.A. "TORCH"

We're here for a reason. I believe a bit of the reason is to throw little torches
out to lead people through the dark. — Whoopi Goldberg

I was nervous about giving a birthday card to someone I didn't know. I thought it was a bit weird and awkward, but afterwards, I felt good. It was nice. I wrote a kind letter to a friend, too, and told him nice things. I was calm before that since I already knew the person. I'm sure it made his day, and I felt great because I did something thoughtful for someone.

For another one of my assignments, I sat next to Tanner, someone I don't usually sit with. Before doing this I was nervous, because I never usually put myself out there. I was also a little scared to do it. I felt uncomfortable at first. After we exchanged a couple of words, things got a little less awkward. After doing this assignment, I felt like a better person. I also felt happy that I made a new friend.

FERIAL PEARSON

JESSICA SWINNERTON - S.K.A. "J. SWINN"

To share often and much ... to know even one life has breathed easier because you have lived. This is to have succeeded. — *Ralph Waldo Emerson*

Well, as a S.K.A. I did nothing that would change the world in a big way, nothing that was extravagant. It was easy and fun. I smiled a whole week at people; they more than likely thought I was crazy, but I knew that maybe it made someone's day a bit brighter. By the end of the week my cheeks hurt so badly, but I felt good about myself. I also wrote an anonymous note to a teacher letting them know they were a good teacher. I chose the most disliked teacher in the school and wrote a thoughtful note saying she was a good teacher for putting up with us crazy teenagers.

The other things I did were just common to me, like talking to a person who was alone, holding a door open for someone, offering my seat to someone old or pregnant, helping people who fell or dropped their books. So, I guess the common thing to do might just make someone smile for that moment.

What I learned from this whole thing is that we all have feelings. Not only do I feel good when someone does something nice for me, but now I know they feel good, too. I might not be the one who changes the world, but I can surely tell you I was a part of something positive. I know that once this "S.K.A." thing stops, I won't. I will keep doing this for as long as I live because it goes back to the simple saying of "treat others the way you want to be treated."

TRISTON HERRING - S.K.A. "TRIS-DOG"

*It is the characteristic of the magnanimous man to ask no favor
but to be ready to do kindness to others. — Aristotle*

Throughout our S.K.A. process, I accomplished several kindness acts — some in secret and some in public. I love doing kind things for others. I feel like it can make someone's day. I sent an anonymous thank you letter to Jesus, because I see him always picking up trash. I stayed after class for two minutes to help clean up the art classroom. People left the room very messy and left markers and papers all over. So I went around and picked them all up. The teacher didn't know that I did the cleaning, but I'm sure that he appreciated it. I felt great after! I felt all warm and cozy and sly, because he had no clue I cleaned up.

I love to do Secret Kindness Acts for teachers because I think that sometimes students give them a hard time. By receiving a Secret Act of Kindness, it might brighten their day. After doing an act of kindness, I feel very happy and proud of myself. I believe people should come together in peace, not with hate. So by doing acts of kindness, you're making someone happy, and no unhappy people means less hate towards one another, which is what I want.

MARLON FERNANDEZ - S.K.A. "BIGGIE"

Tenderness and kindness are not signs of weakness and despair,
but manifestations of strength and resolution. — Kahlil Gibran

I stayed after class to erase my teacher's board. I stayed anyway to try to finish my test, and when I got to my next class, I was late, but I did not care, because I think I made my teacher feel better. I felt happier after that, but not much because I am usually happy.

I wrote a thank you letter to a janitor and included a treat with it. I slipped it in his office without him looking, and I hope he didn't throw it away thinking it was trash without looking at it. I think I made someone's day, but I still feel good, even if he might have thrown it away, because I still did it, and that's what counts.

Sometimes, the kindest thing you can do for someone is show them mercy and forgiveness. If I could teach the world one thing, it would be that.

VICTORIA KASTRUP - S.K.A. "WINGS"

How far that little candle throws his beams!
So shines a good deed in a weary world. — William Shakespeare

My S.K.A. act included looking people in the eyes and smiling for three days. I smiled at everyone. Some looked away, and some smiled back. Also, some gave me a bad look, like I was crazy. Some just stared at me awkwardly, so I looked away, but I felt happier for some reason and I had a mouth that hurt a lot! I became a little less awkward about smiling at people and looking them in the eyes. I liked it, and I think I cheered a few people up. Hopefully, I can do this once in a while to help boost up more people.

I sent an anonymous birthday card, held doors open for people, and each time I did an assignment, I felt happier. It always made my mood better, and I felt more awake.

ALEXIS "LEXI" JOHNSON - S.K.A. "PEANUT"

Great opportunities to help others seldom come, but small ones surround us every day. — Sally Koch

I went to the library for lunch, and there's always this person sitting by themselves, so I sat with them. I was nervous because I didn't know what they were going to do or say, but I was relieved knowing that I could make someone's day better by doing something that was easy for me. It feels great helping someone sitting alone to not feel lonely. It makes me happy knowing that they're happy.

I was always excited for my next assignment, and curious about what it would be. Another time I left a note for one of my teachers, thanking her for everything she does for our class, and all of her hard work. I didn't know how she would respond and when the right time would be to leave it for her, but it worked out. I was so happy because she was excited about the note and it actually meant something to her! I did the same for the attendance lady, for all the times my mom has called me out of class and she let me go to my car with a pass. It feels so good showing people that they actually are appreciated. I would definitely do this again.

KENDRA STORY - S.K.A. "KIKI"

Always be kind, for everyone is fighting a hard battle. — Plato

I made a card that said, "Just for someone special," and brought a piece of candy for the teacher. I was in a bad mood before I put it on her desk. She didn't know it was from me, but I could tell she appreciated it. Doing that simple act put me in a better mood. I ended up feeling a lot happier and better about myself in general. I also left a note and chocolate for the librarians, and I could see they were happy and a little shocked. I was already having a good day, but my day got even better! I even held the door open for another teacher who had full hands, and I could tell she was really surprised. I feel good that I did something nice for someone who appreciated it.

CORRINE COSGROVE - S.K.A. "ANGEL"

Kind words produce their own image in men's souls; and a beautiful image it is.
They soothe and quiet and comfort the hearer. They shame him out of his sour, morose, unkind feelings.
We have not yet begun to use kind words in such abundance as they ought to be used. — Blaise Pascal

It was the end of class, and I knew my S.K.A. act was to stay and help clean up, but I was nervous, worried, and didn't want to help. I stayed and arranged the desks that had been pulled out everywhere. As I was leaving, the teacher thanked me and was grateful for my help. My mood improved, and I felt happy and accomplished.

ALYSSA SCHIRMBECK - S.K.A "SPIRIT"

I have no desire to move mountains, construct monuments, or leave behind in my wake material evidence of my existence. But in the final recollection, if the essence of my being has caused a smile to have appeared upon your face or a touch of joy within your heart ... then in living – I have made my mark. — Thomas L. Odem, Jr.

When Mama Beast came to us with the news that we were able to write a book, I was overjoyed! But I was kind of nervous. I thought about what people would think of me and how it would affect my life, and then I thought to myself, *You know what? It doesn't really matter what people think, in the long run I am going to make others happy, and in return, I will be happy myself.*

My thoughts changed after I completed the first assignment. I loved it! I wrote an anonymous appreciation letter to the janitors. I took it to the office and asked one of the receptionists to put it in a janitor's mailbox. I'm not sure who read it, but I know that I felt really good writing it. I was proud of myself because I don't think anyone really shows appreciation to the janitors, who deserve appreciation and to be recognized for all the hard work they do to keep our school looking the way it does!

My second assignment was to write a thank you note to the librarians and list everything I admired about them. When Mrs. Basye was still our librarian, I wrote an appreciation email to both her and Ms. Sanders because I really enjoyed being in the library and getting to know them. I was a little bit nervous about sending the email because I knew it wouldn't be anonymous but it made me happy to see the smiles on their faces when they thanked me for the email.

On my third assignment I was more at ease with being kind and helpful. I was to help someone who was struggling with homework or class work at least once that week. I helped both my brother and sister with their homework. It was really fun to be reintroduced to things I learned in middle school and in elementary school. I also enjoyed watching them figure out their homework and how happy they were

because they understood it. It also made me proud to have been able to help them!

My fourth assignment was one that my friends and I did but didn't have to. In Avenue Scholars, we have to do "cohorts." Cohorts is like job shadowing and training combined where we go to experience our possible work field. As a reward for completing the cohorts we went skating. It was really fun. Towards the last half hour, the next group came. They were all younger kids who didn't seem to know how to skate. They were so enthusiastic and excited to skate that it rubbed off and we were excited too. The second they hit the skating floor, though, they dropped like flies. I'm not going to lie, it was really funny! A lot of them were having problems skating and my friends Corrine, Maribel, and I knew why. Their skates weren't tied properly. They were so excited to skate they just threw the skates on and said "Let's go!" Corrine and I pulled two kids aside and started tying their skates. Then, more and more kids came. We had about eight kids each. Maribel was helping a little boy to the side so she could help him with his skates as well. The kids were all so adorable, and I admired their effort. After we were all done tying skates, there was an announcement for all Avenue Scholars to leave. We just laughed. We had spent our last half hour tying little children's skates instead of skating like the rest of the Avenue Scholars. It was all worth it!

My fifth assignment is one I did at home. My sister Emily and I are in Completely Kids, formerly known as Campfire USA. We needed 40 hours of community service, so we started thinking of things we could do to help people. Emily and I know that people in nursing homes can get pretty bored and not have a lot of visitors. We also know that children in hospitals can get really sad, so we asked the workers if we could make things for them and help them. We made the kids a lot of melty-bead animals and a tie blanket. It is a lot of work and it can get really boring but it's all worth it to see people smiling and having a good time!

Another time, on my own, I made "Thank You" cards for my teachers. I know they aren't always recognized by students for all the wonderful things they teach us, so I thought it would be nice to make them "Thank You" cards in return for all their hard work and to let them know that they're appreciated.

This last act I recorded was one of the things that made my day. My mom was talking to me about this girl having problems. She said the girl thought she was ugly, people made fun of her, and she tried to commit suicide. I knew who she was talking about. I am a shy person, but I walked right up to the girl and said, "Hi, you are really pretty. I saw you earlier and thought it to myself but figured I'd come up and tell you. If you are going to be here tomorrow, I'd definitely like to come hang out with you!" I made her smile, and it was the greatest thing I have done! I had to leave that night, but I talked to her the next day, and she *is* really nice. I'm glad I met her. Hopefully, what I said to her will make a difference.

The simplest things can make the biggest difference in a person's day. Kindness can spread, one act at a time!

HOW AND WHERE TO FORM
A SECRET KINDNESS AGENT TEAM

When word of our project got out, I started receiving messages from people asking if they could do our project or some version of it. Of course they could, and so can you!

STEP 1

Pick a group, any group, as long as it meets regularly. Here are a few ideas:

- Your family
- Your small or large group of friends
- Your faith community or a committee/group within it
- Your class
- Your school or a committee/group within it
- A club you belong to at school/college/university
- Your neighborhood
- Your book club
- Your gym

- Your sports team
- Your band/symphony/quintet/orchestra/choir
- Your colleagues at work

STEP 2

As a group, decide which place your deeds will affect and limit your acts to that place. It can be as large or as small as you like. If it's your school, all acts should take place within it. For a book club, it could be the neighborhood in which the club meets, or the entire city.

STEP 3

Once you have decided upon your place, create a list of random acts of kindness that you and the people in the group will act upon. Make sure to have as many acts as there are people within the group. You may decide to keep all acts anonymous. If you have trouble coming up with enough ideas, use the ones in this book, or look online; there are hundreds there!

*Be aware that there may be people in your group who could be financially or physically unable to complete certain acts, so be sure not to include any acts that could exclude them.

STEP 4

Decide as a group about the timespan of your project. It could be a month, a year, or indefinite; it's up to your group!

STEP 5

Create your envelopes – one for each act of kindness. Create a list of cheesy songs about social justice. Optional: create an oath and a set of risks.

STEP 6

Every time you meet, take five minutes at the beginning of your meeting to play your cheesy song, pick an envelope, and if you have them, recite your oath and risks. At the end of your meeting, take a few minutes to reflect on any acts of kindness that you have completed, in particular, talk about what happened and how it affected you. You can do this in writing or in discussion, but the reflection is important; it keeps you accountable, reminding you of the good you are doing.

TOP SECRET

AFTERWORD
CARRYING THE NEWS
By Adam Klinker

There's the old adage that no good news ever makes the newspaper. Then, there's what happened in Ferial Pearson's classroom at Ralston High School in the spring of 2013. For that, a newspaper wasn't even necessary, and, by far, it was not the best instrument for broadcasting the simple but immense undertaking of eighteen intrepid students and their indomitable teacher. But the newspaper came, anyway.

I don't remember exactly how I heard about the Secret Kindness Agents. Nobody came right out and said there was such an organization, surreptitiously moving from classroom to classroom, winding through the crush of humanity between periods, tidying up for teachers, sitting down with fellow students they'd never met and striking up conversations, and dropping off little mini-grants to kids they saw striving but struggling. Though I learned later that Ferial had planned this as a semester-long project—complete with assignments and a journaling component—the whole idea struck me as quite organic. After all, even the farmer who sows a field with seed and then leaves that field alone, will see a crop come through for seasons to come. What I do recall was the echo of so many teachers and students and aides and custodians at Ralston High who recounted for me what was happening in the halls. It was not the usual hijinks and buffeting that comes with the well-traveled teenage territory that lies between rows

of lockers and non-descript classroom doors. It was not the innate adolescent cynicism in the face of true kindness. And it was not struck through with the kind of cosseting that any freshman can sniff out in an instant. Something palpable was changing for the better at Ralston. Even the hardest-shelled high-schooler was not immune to this sudden burst of new, positive energy.

All this led me to Ferial's classroom one April day, where the Secret Kindness Agents, a little reluctantly, revealed their true identities, and told me of their mission. They were, after all, attempting to effect a change in the culture at Ralston, something not easily done in any school. But in the wake of the tragedy at Sandy Hook Elementary School the previous December, with all corners exclaiming "What is to be done?" here were these kids, doing something. The idea was simple: what if one simple act of kindness could turn someone's day, attitude, life, in another direction? Like the do-gooders of old, the agents clapped erasers, they tidied up desk rows, and they threw away garbage. But they also went through the halls grinning broadly at everyone they encountered. They said hello to the quiet kid, and they asked the name of the girl nobody knows. They offered part of their lunch to the boy who wasn't eating. What started as a secret soon became a roar.

But again, the acts seemed so small an offering to make. As Maribel Navarrete put it to me, "A lot of people say, 'Don't sweat the small stuff,' and I've never understood why. The small things often make the most difference in a person's life. A small crack in a foundation can lead to major problems." I found her metaphor more than apt. The Secret Kindness Agents were, in a manner of speaking, rebuilding the way they and their teachers and peers, looked at the world.

As the local newspaper reporter, I was familiar with most of the students in the Avenue Scholars program. I'd encountered them in various other guises as poets, club presidents, and activists. These were kids from every walk of the highly-stratified high school society. And here they were, cutting across the sacrosanct boundaries to practice random and sometimes not-so-random acts, from the heart, to the betterment of their school and themselves. What struck me was not the typical high-school demurrals that I encounter when I ask the youth about their feats, but rather the quiet certainty they each possessed. They

knew what they were doing. They took pride in it. But they did not deem it necessary to shout it from the rooftops. These builders of the new world understood that it's the relatively few who get headlines. It's the many who do the work. Being about the business of doing good on this earth resided well in them. Here were thousands of years of wisdom alighting on the young: that if every act we undertake in this plane of existence has its equal echo in some other place, at some other time, let that echo be one resounding with peace and light.

And that's the very definition of good news.

TOP SECRET

FINAL WORD

It's been a year since we started our project, and although I'm not their teacher anymore, I have stayed in touch with my Secret Kindness Agents. They continue to tell me about simple acts of kindness they see, experience, or complete on their own. A few months ago, Mackenzie showed up, randomly, on my doorstep with a thoughtful "Thank You" card and some chocolates, and it meant the world to me. When I asked her what she had been doing in the past year, she said, "I just leave little notes for people saying how much they're appreciated. When it was snowing I scraped people's windshields and left a note with 'Secret Kindness Agents' on it. I paid for a lady's groceries the other day. That wasn't so secret, but it meant something to her. I like that it means something to other people. Maybe it will make them believe there is good still out there."

This was so important to me because "Cheezy" doesn't even go to the same school anymore and continues with our project.

I asked a few of the Agents what their thoughts are about the project now and I should have known that their responses would make my face hurt from smiling so much. Ayele said the project taught her she should follow her heart, and so she doesn't let anyone or anything bring her down anymore. She feels that she is way stronger than she thought she was. This meant a lot to me, because Ayele was so afraid of completing the assignments at first. She was terrified of people laughing at her, and when they did she

would be devastated. Her newly found self-confidence makes me so happy.

Kashya said doing the project made her feel like a weight had been taken from her shoulders because it was the right thing to do. She felt good because she knew she didn't spend her junior year messing around; she actually did something to make someone's day better. She still keeps her eye out for opportunities to be kind. Ernie said, "I've been more calm and relaxed with people now. It has become a lot easier for me to simply just talk to someone and build a small friendship because I try and help that person. In a way I'm still doing the acts of kindness, but now they're happening unconsciously." Jesus added, "I would have to agree and say that now instead of waiting for our next assignment, we do them unconsciously, and I don't ever expect anything from them. It's just plain kindness."

Throughout our time together, I watched my Baby Beasts become family to each other. I watched them lift each other up when someone was down, celebrate each other's accomplishments, and smile bravely through tears. One of my Agents attempted suicide fourteen times before he got to my class; he flourishes now and walks with his head held high and his eyes open to the opportunities to help others.

Kindness gave us hope, which squashed anger in my students and the sense of futility in me. It gave us a sense of purpose as a group as well as individually. It created allies in us and quiet defenders of the bullied, and it gave us all the courage to take a deep breath and do something small, having no idea about the impact of our actions. Most importantly, it helped to lift the veil of darkness that surrounds personal and global tragedies.

Someone once told me that there is a difference between pain and suffering. Pain comes when terrible things happen, but suffering comes from wishing the past could have been different. We cannot avoid pain, but we do have a choice as to whether or not we suffer; instead of wishing painful things had never happened, we can work to prevent tragedies in the future. I hope you choose not to suffer, and I hope this book gives you the tools to make that happen.

— Ferial Pearson

TOP SECRET

APPENDIX
For Teachers and Educators
National Teaching Standards

This project addresses some National Curriculum or Teaching Standards, particularly in the areas of Social Studies and Language Arts. Teachers can use their creativity and expertise to tweak the project to be appropriate for various grade levels, weaving it into existing Social Studies units on Individual Development and Identity and Civic Ideals and Practices or into at least seven of the twelve National Language Arts Standards listed here.

As all good teachers know, reflection is key in learning, whether it happens through written or spoken dialogue. Since no two classrooms are the same, and since only a teacher will know his or her students' contexts, the project will not develop the same in each classroom or school; teachers and school administrators should mold this project to fit the needs of their own students, and I strongly urge that reflection happens weekly, at the very least. This can be done in whole group discussion, small group or paired conversations, quick journaling, or more formal writing. It doesn't have to take long, but the result is powerful, even if accomplished in five minutes.

Of course, most schools also have a code of conduct. In my children's school and in the schools in which I have taught, students are told to "Be Safe, Be Respectful, Be Responsible." This project is a great way to teach those behaviors as well.

Social Studies – Taken from The National Council for the Social Studies
http://www.socialstudies.org/standards/strands

Theme 4: Individual Development and Identity
  The study of individual development and identity will help students to describe factors important to the development of personal identity. They will explore the influence of peoples, places, and environments on personal development. Students will hone personal skills such as demonstrating self-direction when working towards and accomplishing personal goals, and making an effort to understand others and their beliefs, feelings, and convictions.

  In the early grades, young learners develop their personal identities in the context of families, peers, schools, and communities. Central to this development are the exploration, identification, and analysis of how individuals and groups are alike and how they are unique, as well as how they relate to each other in supportive and collaborative ways.

  In the middle grades, issues of personal identity are refocused as the individual begins to explain his or her unique qualities in relation to others, collaborates with peers and with others, and studies how individuals develop in different societies and cultures.

  At the high school level, students need to encounter multiple opportunities to examine contemporary patterns of human behavior, using methods from the behavioral sciences to apply core concepts drawn from psychology, sociology, and anthropology as they apply to individuals, societies, and cultures.

Theme 10: Civic Ideals and Practices
  Questions faced by students studying this theme might be: What are the democratic ideals and

practices of a constitutional democracy? What is the balance between rights and responsibilities? What is civic participation? How do citizens become involved? What is the role of the citizen in the community and the nation, and as a member of the world community?

Students will explore how individuals and institutions interact. They will also recognize and respect different points of view. Students learn by experience how to participate in community service and political activities and how to use democratic processes to influence public policy.

In schools, this theme typically appears in units or courses dealing with civics, history, political science, cultural anthropology, and fields such as global studies and law-related education, while also drawing upon content from the humanities.

In the early grades, students are introduced to civic ideals and practices through activities such as helping to set classroom expectations, examining experiences in relation to ideals, participating in mock elections, and determining how to balance the needs of individuals and the group. During these years, children also experience views of citizenship in other times and places through stories and drama.

By the middle grades, students expand their knowledge of democratic ideals and practices, along with their ability to analyze and evaluate the relationships between these ideals and practices. They are able to see themselves taking civic roles in their communities.

High school students increasingly recognize the rights and responsibilities of citizens in identifying societal needs, setting directions for public policies, and working to support both individual dignity and the common good. They become familiar with methods of analyzing important public issues and evaluating different recommendations for dealing with these issues.

Language Arts Standards - Taken from The National Council of Teachers of English
http://www.ncte.org/standards/ncte-ira

Standard 4

Students adjust their use of spoken, written, and visual language (e.g., conventions, style, vocabulary) to communicate effectively with a variety of audiences and for different purposes.

Standard 5

Students employ a wide range of strategies as they write and use different writing process elements appropriately to communicate with different audiences for a variety of purposes

Standard 7

Students conduct research on issues and interests by generating ideas and questions, and by posing problems. They gather, evaluate, and synthesize data from a variety of sources to communicate their discoveries in ways that suit their purpose and audience.

Standard 9

Students develop an understanding of and respect for diversity in language use, patterns, and dialects across cultures, ethnic groups, geographic regions, and social roles.

Standard 10

Students whose first language is not English make use of their first language to develop competency in the English Language Arts and to develop understanding of content across the curriculum.

FERIAL PEARSON

Standard 11

Students participate as knowledgeable, reflective, creative, and critical members of a variety of literacy communities.

Standard 12

Students use spoken, written, and visual language to accomplish their own purposes (e.g., for learning, enjoyment, persuasion, and the exchange of information.

ABOUT THE AUTHOR
Ferial Pearson
S.K.A. "Mama Beast"

Ferial Pearson was born and raised in Nairobi, Kenya. She is the oldest of four girls and the first in her immediate family to go to college. After graduating from Peponi School in 1997, she left Africa to attend Gustavus Adolphus College in Saint Peter, Minnesota, where in 2001 she earned her Bachelor's Degree in Communication Arts Literature Teaching, and where she met her husband, Daniel. She was offered the opportunity to teach in the Omaha Public School District at South High School that fall, where she taught English and Reading. During her time there, she also served as the Gay Straight Alliance and Unity Club sponsor, and received national awards for her work with students and in the community. These included the National Education Association's Virginia Uribe Award for Creative Leadership in Human Rights in 2012, the Gay Lesbian Straight Education Network's Educator of the Year Respect Award in 2011, and she was the Nebraska representative and finalist for the National Council of Teachers of English Academic Freedom Award in 2012. Locally, she has been awarded the 2011 Omaha Education Association's Human Relations Award, the 2012 Promising Professional Award from the University of Nebraska at Omaha, and RESPECT's 2011 Anti-Bullying Award. She also earned her Master's degree in Curriculum and Instruction with a Graduate Certificate in Urban Instruction from the University of

Nebraska at Omaha in 2009.

Ferial left Omaha South High School in 2011 to work as a Talent Advisor for the Avenue Scholars Foundation and taught for them at Ralston High School for two years until 2013, during which time she created the Secret Kindness Agents project with her junior class. She now works as an Instructor and Instructional Coach at the University of Nebraska at Omaha in the Teacher Education Department and is working on her doctorate in Educational Leadership. She lives in Ralston, Nebraska with her husband Daniel, son Ilahi, and daughter Iman. Together, they do random acts of kindness every day.

ACKNOWLEDGEMENTS

I am privileged to have so many supportive and inspirational people in my life who have helped me in my journey of writing this book, as small as it is.

The Secret Kindness Agents, A.K.A., My Baby Beasts

My soul mate Dan, my son Ilahi, and my daughter Iman

My parents, Ghalib and Fiza; my sisters Aliya, Yasmin, and Salma; and my Grandparents

My IncluCity Family at Inclusive Communities who know who they are and are too many to list here

WriteLife, and in particular, Cindy Grady and Erin Reel

Sarah Edwards and Jennifer Hensel

Dan Boster

Adam Klinker and the Ralston Recorder

The University of Nebraska at Omaha and the fabulous faculty (now also my friends)

FERIAL PEARSON

Faculty and Staff of Ralston High School and in particular, Shannon Lewis, Cassie's Envelope Genius, my office mate Maria Weaver, Gay Straight Alliance sponsor Jennifer Stark, and Jonatha Basye the librarian

My coworkers at The Avenue Scholars Foundation - www.avescholars.org

Warren Whitted, Sophia Jackson, Cathy Grondek, Christiana Bratiotis, Joni Stacy, Marianne Laski, and Jan Duren for contributing to Cassie's Envelopes